Numeral

J. Baptiste

Also by J. Baptiste

First Time Homebuyer Gold

One for the Tenant

Coming Soon

One for the Landlord

Numeral M

First Stillwater River Publications Edition.

ISBN: 978-1-963296-36-5

1 2 3 4 5 6 7 8 9 10
Written by J. Baptiste.
Cover & interior book design by Matthew St. Jean.
Published by Stillwater River Publications,
West Warwick, RI, USA.

Names: Baptiste, J., author. Title: Numeral M / J. Baptiste.
Description: First Stillwater River Publications edition. | West Warwick, RI,
    USA : Stillwater River Publications, [2024.]
Identifiers: ISBN: 978-1-963296-23-5 (paperback)
Subjects: LCSH: Finance, Personal. | Saving and investment. | Thriftiness.
Classification: LCC: HG179 .B36 2024 | DDC: 332.024—dc23

*This book is dedicated to
all my readers for your continued support!
Thank you!*

◆ ◆ ◆

Contents

Introduction

Hello, my readers!

Thank you so very much for joining me on another awesome read. I have received a lot of requests to write a book detailing how to save money in a simplified way. These requests stemmed from the savings section in my *One for the Tenant* book.

This book will provide two different approaches to saving a specified amount. Many people do not believe that with their current income, it will ever be possible for them to save a substantial amount or any money at all.

With the steps in this book, you will see that you can save, but you will need to cut back on unnecessary spending and put on the armor of discipline when spending. This book provides you with actual figures (there are many more ways, but these I chose to put together) to demonstrate that it can be done. I believe in providing visuals to my readers which in turn will allow them to take the reins of their savings goals. Each section provides exercises on how to accomplish the approach, techniques to use (all in or split it), and a savings outlook, which acts as a summary. *You can begin using these savings techniques at any time using a year containing 52 weeks.*

I chose to use the roman numeral "M" to outline this book. Anytime you see the term "M" know that it refers to its meaning of 1,000 and you are trying to reach that "M" goal. *For the purposes in this book, specific monetary denominations will be used but you can use whatever denominations you like.*

Everyone is different, so try the approach and techniques that best fit your needs. From the Table of Contents, pick one or more of the amounts that you would like to aim towards saving. I want you to challenge yourself throughout the year to reach it. Remember to never limit yourself!

Ready?

Let's get started!

$20.00 (Split It) Approach to $1,040

For this approach we will use what I call the "split it" approach. Some people do not like to look at it as an entire $20.00 bill, so by splitting it into smaller denominations, it may not look as daunting. In this particular exercise, we will use two deposits of $10.00.

We will use the year 2024, which is 52 weeks long. Calculations are based on a weekly pay period.

"Split it" exercise:
- Two regular savings accounts (Account A and Account B) are opened at the local financial institution.
- Set aside $20.00 from every paycheck received.
- Have the $20.00 split two ways. Either automatically or manually deposit
  - » $10.00 into savings Account A.
  - » $10.00 into savings Account B.
- Repeat this with every paycheck you receive for the year.

That's it! Try not to withdraw any funds from these accounts!

Savings Outlook

To summarize:
- At the beginning of the year, it is decided $20.00 will be set aside from every weekly paycheck.
- The decided funds are split every pay period by adding $10.00 to Savings Account A, and $10.00 to Savings Account B.
- At the end of the year, if the two accounts remained untouched with no withdrawals, savings account A will have a balance of $520.00, and savings account B will have a balance of $520.00

When the totals of both accounts are added together, there will be a saved total for the year of $1,040.00. You did it!

Just like that you've saved and reached the "M" goal!

Small beginnings are beautiful ones!

Congratulations!

$20.00 (All In) Approach to $1,040

If you decide that the "all in" approach works better for you to reach the "M" goal at the end of the year, then let's get started! For this approach, we will use what I call the "all in" approach.

We will use the year 2024 which is 52 weeks long. Calculations are based on a weekly pay period.

"All in" exercise:
- One regular savings account (Account C) is opened at a local financial institution.
- Set aside $20.00 from every paycheck received.
- Have the $20.00 either automatically or manually deposited into savings account C.
- Repeat this with every paycheck you receive for the year.

That's it! Try not to withdraw any funds from this account!

Savings Outlook

To summarize:

- At the beginning of the year, it is decided $20.00 will be set aside from every weekly paycheck.
- The funds are deposited weekly into savings account C.
- At the end of the year, if account C remains untouched with no withdrawals, it will have a balance of $1,040.00.

You did it! Just like that you just saved and reached the "M" goal!

You got this!

Keep going!

$30.00 (Split It) Approach to $1,560

For this approach we will use what I call the "split it" approach. Some people do not like to look at it as $30.00, so by splitting it into smaller denominations, it may not look as challenging.

In this particular exercise, we will deposit $15.00 into each account.

We will use the year 2024, which has 52 weeks. Calculations are based on a weekly pay period.

"Split it" exercise:
- Two regular savings accounts (Account D and Account E) are opened at a local financial institution .
- Set aside $30.00 from every paycheck received.
- Have the $30.00 split two ways, and either automatically or manually deposit
  » $15.00 into savings Account D
  » $15.00 into savings Account E
- Repeat this with every paycheck you receive for the year.

That's it! Try not to withdraw any funds from these accounts!

Savings Outlook

To summarize:
- At the beginning of the year, it is decided $30.00 will be set aside from every *weekly* paycheck.
- The funds are split every pay period by adding $15.00 to Savings Account D, and $15.00 to Savings Account E.
- At the end of the year, if both accounts remained untouched with no withdrawals, savings account D will have a balance of $780.00, and savings account E will have a balance of $780.00.

When the totals of both accounts are added together, there is a saved total for the year of $1,560.00. You did it!

Just like that you just exceeded the "M" goal!

Awesome!

$30.00 (All In) Approach to $1,560

If you decide that the "all in" approach works better for you to reach the "M" goal at the end of the year, let's get started! For this approach we will use the "all in" approach.

We will use the year 2024, which is 52 weeks long. Calculations are based on a weekly pay period.

"All in" exercise:
- One regular savings account (Account F) is opened at a local financial institution .
- Set aside $30.00 from every paycheck received.
- Have the $30.00 either automatically or manually deposited into savings account F.
- Repeat this with every paycheck you receive for the year.

That's it! Try not to withdraw any funds from this account!

Savings Outlook

To summarize:

- At the beginning of the year, it is decided $30.00 will be set aside from every weekly paycheck.
- The funds are deposited into savings account F.
- At the end of the year, if account F remains untouched with no withdrawals it will have a balance of $1,560.

You're challenging yourself to continue increasing your saving goals. Great job!

Congratulations!

$40.00 (Split It) Approach to $2,080

For this approach we will use what I call the "split it" approach. Some people do not like to look at it as an entire $40.00, so by splitting it into smaller denominations, it may not look as hard to accomplish.

For this particular exercise, we will use two deposits of $20.00.

We will use the year 2024, which is 52 weeks long. Calculations are based on a weekly pay period.

"Split it" exercise:
- Two regular savings accounts (Account G and Account H) are opened at a local financial institution.
- Set aside $40.00 from every paycheck received.
- Have the $40.00 split two ways. Either automatically or manually deposit
  » $20.00 into savings Account G.
  » $20.00 into savings Account H.
- Repeat this with every weekly paycheck you receive for the year.

That's it! Try not to withdraw any funds from these accounts!

Savings Outlook

To summarize:
- At the beginning of the year, it is decided $40.00 will be set aside from every weekly paycheck.
- The decided funds are split every pay period by adding $20.00 to Savings Account G, and $20.00 to Savings Account H.
- At the end of the year, if both accounts remained untouched with no withdrawals, savings account G will have a balance of $1,040.00, and savings account H will have a balance of $1,040.00

When the totals of all 2 accounts have been added together, there is a saved total for the year of $2,080.00. Awesome!

You're getting good at this!

$40.00 (All In) Approach to $2,080

If you decide that the "all in" approach works better for you to reach and exceed the "M" goal at the end of the year, let's get started! For this approach we will use the "all in" approach.

We will use the year 2024, which is 52 weeks long. Calculations are based on a weekly pay period.

"All in" exercise:
- One regular savings account (Account I) is opened at a local financial institution .
- Set aside $40.00 from every paycheck received.
- Have the $40.00 either automatically or manually deposited into savings account I.
- Repeat this with every paycheck you receive for the year.

That's it! Try not to withdraw any funds from this account!

Savings Outlook

To summarize:
- At the beginning of the year, it is decided $40.00 will be set aside from every weekly paycheck.
- The funds are deposited into savings account I.
- At the end of the year, if account I remained untouched with no withdrawals, it will have a balance of $2,080.00.

Excellent Job!

$80.00 (Split It) Approach to $4,160

For this approach we will use the "split it" approach. Some people do not like to look at it as an entire $80.00, so by splitting it into smaller denominations, it may look more manageable.

We will use the year 2024, which is 52 weeks long. Calculations are based on a weekly pay period.

"Split it" exercise:
- Two regular savings accounts (Account J and Account K) are opened at a local financial institution.
- Set aside $80.00 from every paycheck received.
- Have the $80.00 split two ways. Either automatically or manually deposit
  - » $40.00 into savings Account J
  - » $40.00 into savings Account K
- Repeat this with every paycheck you receive for the year.

That's it! Try not to withdraw any funds from these accounts!

Savings Outlook

To summarize:
- At the beginning of the year, it is decided $80.00 will be set aside from every paycheck.
- The decided funds are split every pay period by adding $40.00 to Savings Account J, and $40.00 to Savings Account K.
- At the end of the year, if both accounts remained untouched with no withdrawals, savings account J will have a balance of $2,080.00, and savings account K will have a balance of $2,080.00

When the totals of both accounts have been added together, there is a saved total for the year of $4,160.00. Awesome!

WOW! Major accomplishment!

$80.00 (All In) Approach to $4,160

If you decide that the "all in" approach works better for you to reach and exceed the "M" goal by the end of the year, let's get started!

We will use the year 2024, which is 52 weeks long. Calculations are based on a weekly pay period.

"All in" exercise:
- One regular savings account (Account L) is opened at the local financial institution .
- Set aside 80.00 from every paycheck received.
- Have the $80.00 either automatically or manually deposited into savings account L.
- Repeat this with every paycheck you receive for the year.

That's it! Try not to withdraw any funds from this account!

Savings Outlook

To summarize:
- At the beginning of the year, it is decided $80.00 will be set aside from every weekly paycheck.
- The funds are deposited into savings account L.
- At the end of the year, if account L remained untouched with no withdrawals, it will have a balance of $4,160.

Superb!

$100.00 (Split It) Approach to $5,200

For this example, we will use the "split it" approach. Some people do not like to look at it as an entire $100.00, so by splitting it into smaller denominations it may not look as intimidating .

We will use the year 2024, which has 52 weeks. Calculations are based on a weekly pay period.

"Split it" exercise:
- Two regular savings accounts (Account M and Account N) are opened at the local financial institution .
- Set aside $100.00 from every paycheck received.
- Have the $100.00 split two ways and either automatically or manually deposit
  - » $50.00 into savings Account M.
  - » $50.00 into savings Account N.
- Repeat this with every weekly paycheck you receive for the year.

That's it! Try not to withdraw any funds from these accounts!

Savings Outlook

To summarize:

- At the beginning of the year, it is decided that $100.00 will be set aside from every weekly paycheck.
- The funds are split every pay period by adding $50.00, to Savings Account M, and $50.00 to Savings Account N.
- At the end of the year, if both accounts remained untouched with no withdrawals, savings account M will have a balance of $2,600 and savings account N will have a balance of $2,600.

When the totals of both accounts have been added together, there is a saved total for the year of $5,200.00.

Ask yourself: how does this accomplishment feel?

Massive!

$100.00 (All In) Approach to $5,200

If you decide that the "all in" approach works better for you to reach and exceed the "M" goal by the end of the year let's get started!

We will use the year 2024, which is 52 weeks long. Calculations are based on a weekly pay period.

"All in" exercise:
- One regular savings account (Account O) is opened at a local financial institution .
- Set aside 100.00 from every paycheck received.
- Have the $100.00 either automatically or manually deposited into savings account O.
- Repeat this with every paycheck you receive for the entire year.

That's it! Try not to withdraw any funds from this account!

Savings Outlook

To summarize:
- At the beginning of the year it is decided $100.00 will be set aside from every weekly paycheck.
- The funds are deposited into savings account O.
- At the end of the year, if account O remained untouched with no withdrawals, it will have a balance of $5,200.

Blessings to you for making it this far and accomplishing more than the "M" goal!

Cheers!

Best Wishes!

The subject matter in this book was designed to give you actual ways to save specific amounts of money. The material in this book in no way should be substituted for legal or financial advice. There are many different ways to save, and each person's need for saving is different. Remember to do what works for you. I decided to use the year 2024, but you can use the savings techniques in this book and start any time you decide. It doesn't matter when you start using the savings tips, but the best time to attempt it would be the beginning of the year. Remember these tips will help you to save over the "M" goal depending on which technique you use.

Discipline is definitely key! This book contains no gimmicks or tricks, just more plain (simple) actual figures on ways to save.

As always, I keep my books short but detailed for better clarification and understanding. The balances in the savings accounts used in the exercises are before compound interest is added by the financial institution. Again, if I am able to help just one person by providing them with techniques on how to begin saving and bettering themselves, this book was worth writing.

Remember to save, no matter how small the amount you put aside each time. It will surprise you that you can accomplish it!

Blessings to you!

Thank you for your continued support and see you on the next exciting read!